Preface

Deep End was never meant to be a book. It started as pages torn from moments, quiet ones, painful ones, the kind you write down just to survive. These words lived in journals, phone notes, and late-night thoughts. For a long time, they were only for me.

But somewhere along the way, I realized that what I felt wasn't just mine. That the silence I was writing through might echo in someone else's story too.

So I gathered the pieces, not to create something perfect, but to offer something honest. These poems are the result of giving myself permission, to feel fully, to fall apart, to question love, and to search for meaning in the mess.

This is not a guidebook. It's a mirror. A collection of quiet confessions, soul scribbles, and unspoken endings. A diary turned offering.

If you've ever kept something inside because you didn't know how to say it out loud—I wrote this for you.

With love,

Duyusime

Table Of Content

Life jacket

Trying to stay afloat with a life jacket filled with sand; given to me by the one who would never watch me drown.

He watched with tears in his eyes as my body sank, too tangled to set myself free.

He loved me enough, but not more than his own Survival.

Clear

Love will justify every doubting action
even when the evidence is clear.

Feels

It feels like heartbreak

A quiet quake beneath my skin,

Shaking me gently back to a truth I've

buried.

Like ancient rocks colliding, then parting,

Cracking open with purpose,

They leave behind layers of beauty

Each one a silent witness

To the shifting, shaping,

Becoming.

Insane

I am only insane if you choose insanity
So don't disturbed my solitude.
We can both make a decision and end up

here,
but this is the last time, I swear.
I will choose the same path no matter how
dark and treacherous.
The journey was beautiful, even in all the
chaos that came after.
I choose you which is insane.
The sane mind can detach and expect nothing
less.

I need sanity to understand that to choose me
means not repeating your past actions.

Spin Cycle

In a spin cycle, the chaos doesn't seem as terrible
as it truly is.

If you focus just enough on a single point,
the turmoil fades, and calmness takes over.
While spinning, it all becomes one

but it is at the moment you try to regain stability
that the world begins to turn upside down.
Slowing down reveals the quiet collapse of everything
you knew.

Recognizing that it is as bad as it seems,
sifting through the wreckage to save what you
can.
Only then, will you truly understand what is
worth keeping and to let what cannot be
saved.

Solemate, and Codependency

Somewhere between soulmate and
codependency, I Ican't seem to find my place.
A soulmate is someone you meet, no matter
when and no matter where, makes a moment feel
like forever.
The person who gives you grace when you need it
most.
The one who brings you back to your truest self,
without a facade.
The person you love most, who chooses you fully
and without hesitation

Yet with all its beauty is the daunting feeling that
To walk away, even briefly, feels paralyzing.
It is wanting not to choose, but falling in and out
of love,
Questioning whether it's destiny... or
dependency

Take a seat

Take a seat while I hand you my burden.
Take a seat while I draw back the curtain.
Listen as I spill. My cup has overflowed,
            yet I feel empty.

Can you tell I've got plenty on my mind?
To choose between love or where I belong.
To choose between the life I was destined to have
    or to give it all up for a love I never had.

Take a seat, it won't take long.
I must get these words out
to let the weight off my tongue.

Tell me there is more behind the madness.
I am doing all the right things
but I see no writing on the walls.

A blank canvas for a story I am trying to create.
Now it is a plot I hate.
My thoughts led me astray
without a way to navigate.
So now I'm here.
Thank you for listening.
Now let's erase those moments
and go back to pretending

Let It Go

Let it go. Your perception has been fractured. I
promise,
they don't hate you.
They simply can't bear the thought
that they aren't whole enough to be what you
deserve.
Forgive them for your own peace.
They never had the chance
to heal from wounds that existed long before you
arrived.
Your reality becomes clouded
when doubt is poured into your path by others.
Forgive them.
They've never walked in your shoes.
Forgive them so you can create the reality you
deserve
and leave them behind,
along with their pain and unhealed past.

Cycle

It feels like a never-ending cycle, just getting by.
Waking up, showing up, pushing forward through
days that blur into each other. We all know it's only a
matter of time. My sources? Those who came before
me. A story told a million times.
The irony is, time is a resource, and for every human,
it is limited.
Everything must align perfectly, because when it's
finally my time to fully understand all you've ever
told me, your clock will have run out. That's the
tragedy of time. We don't always get to share the
clarity.

The cycle of life it is both painless and painful. Still, we keep moving. We keep listening. We keep trying to understand, even when we're running out of time.

Recreated

You will be my demise. I say it once, twice, and again, around the curve of the moon. You are my demise.

I love you too much to disappoint. But I hate you enough to walk away. I trust you enough to hand you my heart . But I breathe regret. In every inhale, in every pause between "what if" and "too late."

It's in the air, woven into every decision I've made, decisions that never felt fully mine.

Because you took so much of me, stripped away the pieces I once called self.

And now, I question everything.

Was I born for this? Made to orbit your needs, to bend, to break, to become what you needed even when it broke me?

I feel like I was created not for me, but for you. To serve your purpose. And in doing so, I vanished.

Love

You either love me enough to change,
or I love you enough to do the same.

If we are both already who we are meant to be,
then maybe we are not meant for each other.

But if we are,
we will both adapt and become better.
The end.

Regret

Do you know the things I've done?

My lips cannot part to speak the actions of my past self.

I try to hide those actions on the shelves,

behind the books filled with tears that others have shed.

I am far from perfection,

but it is impossible to open the doors I have sealed.

I have grown,

but it takes a level of strength to look them in the face,

knowing how deeply my words once hurt.

I know I am forgiven,
but that alone is not enough.
Self-forgiveness is the hardest kind of pressure
it feels like your entire existence has turned to dust.

The hurt I caused was not fair to my victims.
Stepping outside of my own ego,
I see the pain I caused was only a reflection
of the wounds once inflicted upon me.

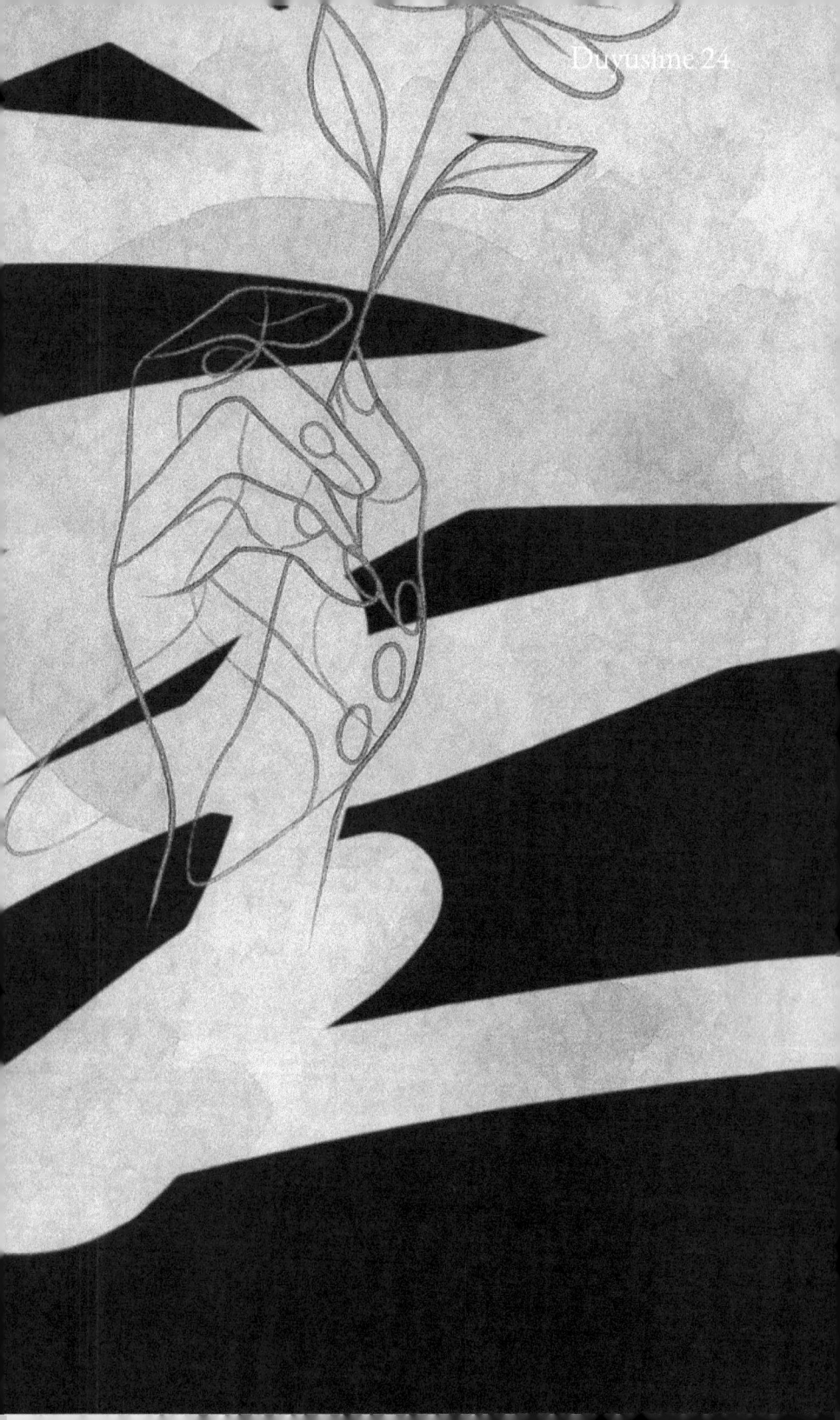

Push X Pull

You push, I pull that is our dynamic
Are you afraid of being hurt?
Do you fear showing your love for it not to be
enough?
Have you gotten used to the easy things being
rough?

When it's easy it is hard when it's good you
expect something bad.

You want to be loved in a way that isn't
questionable.

Yet I show you love and the roles are
reversed. You become a cold heart with a
bitter pride

What am I to do? We push, we pull but one day the tension will break the rope that holds us in place.

So if I pull let me fall into your arms or let me go so I can be the one for another .

I have secrets

I have secrets, none that I would like to tell.
The type of secret so deep and dark
A black hole of emotions that most cannot
bear.

I have secrets, secrets I never knew I had
stories of my friends never to be told.

I hold so much in a bearer of it all and I fear
when I no longer can hold its weights.

I have secrets and it has become me
I am the secret

Remembering when most have

forgotten.

What is was

Is it your guilt over how you treated me? Is it
regret for never once defending me?
The world may never know, but I always will.
Tell me your story, without changing the
narrative. Don't dress it up with a bow or twist it
into something noble.
Just give me one genuine reason why your anger
was so direct. You sharpened your arrows and
aimed them at my neck.
Was it hate? Was it envy? Was it easier to hurt me
than to face yourself?
I think about itall of it. And just know, I
remember. It was a quiet November. When all is
said, it has already been done.

Days alone

Days alone are hurricane eyes pearling
from above.

Days alone are white walls and static
screens filled with inner screams.

Days alone is a room filled with
endless space.

Days alone are never lonely because
thoughts are Loud.

Days alone are harmonic
melancholy bouncing off my ear-
drums.

Closer

Come a little closer let my soft voice
whisper, Hear me whimper because he took
my innocence.

Don't be alarmed by my tears. I'm just a
little girl .I know I stand tall with my might
and all but here I am a child waiting to tell.
Can you hear me?

Can I tell you a secret I kept too long. one
that is the center of my nightmares; I no
longer dream.

The secret is I am no longer whole
 a part of me is turned upside down while
everyone around me is ignoring all the signs.

Signs painted in red, stop please.

He is not who you think he is, Please don't
leave Because when you're gone there's only
me.

Can I tell you a secret ?
I already have, the blank stares behind my
eyes is the only honesty that exists but the
guilt in his eyes is bypassed by his smile.

if you look close enough is a little girl still

laying there wondering of the clouds ignoring

the inner screams.

Past or Present

Looking back on the past;
Is looking at a broken mirror ,
You either remember the joy experienced
before the horror or become fixated on moment of
deep sorrow.

Looking at the past gives you hope,
Still it can shatter your perception.

Reality is not what you see
It is already happening.

You can choose to reflect on what is still
broken and understand it's Beauty

Or be stuck on the distorted reflection while life passes you by.

The fracture cannot be undone.

Maybe Never

I refuse to make it easy to love me,
I fear it will only be for a moment,
A moment that feels like eternity.

I disagree, hoping you will eventually
understand that I do believe all that you speak
to me.

I will not trust that you have given your all
Doing so means I have to give you mine.

I deny that you can be mine forever; that is understanding that death exists and I will never be alone again.

I will never show you my heart,
An opportunity to unplug that which keeps me breathing .

I will not be swept off my feet , then you will become my pavement.
The panic of being brought to my knees to never stand again Keeps me alive.

How can I possibly give that away?

Momentarily

I love you for who I am at that moment I
cannot love who I will become one day.

Love is quite spiteful and selfish, a potion
quite potent.

Today you hold my hand while I cry I give
you all I have, my emotions get away.

We are pieces of puzzles that fit perfectly, We
talk about dreams, the person we hope to be.

My love for you is conditional; It's
unfortunate how it has changed.

Not a spur of the moment decision, not all at once. I wish I could give you more with the time that has passed but..

Today I do not love you; even so my heart aches for the feelings I know I had.

Step Out

The days that challenge your person are the worst. When you realize the person you want to be is the complete opposite of who you are.

The push to break the bubble that has concealed you from hurt, rejection and self hatred.

The same bubble that keeps you from growing and showing your greatest potential.

Duyusime 44

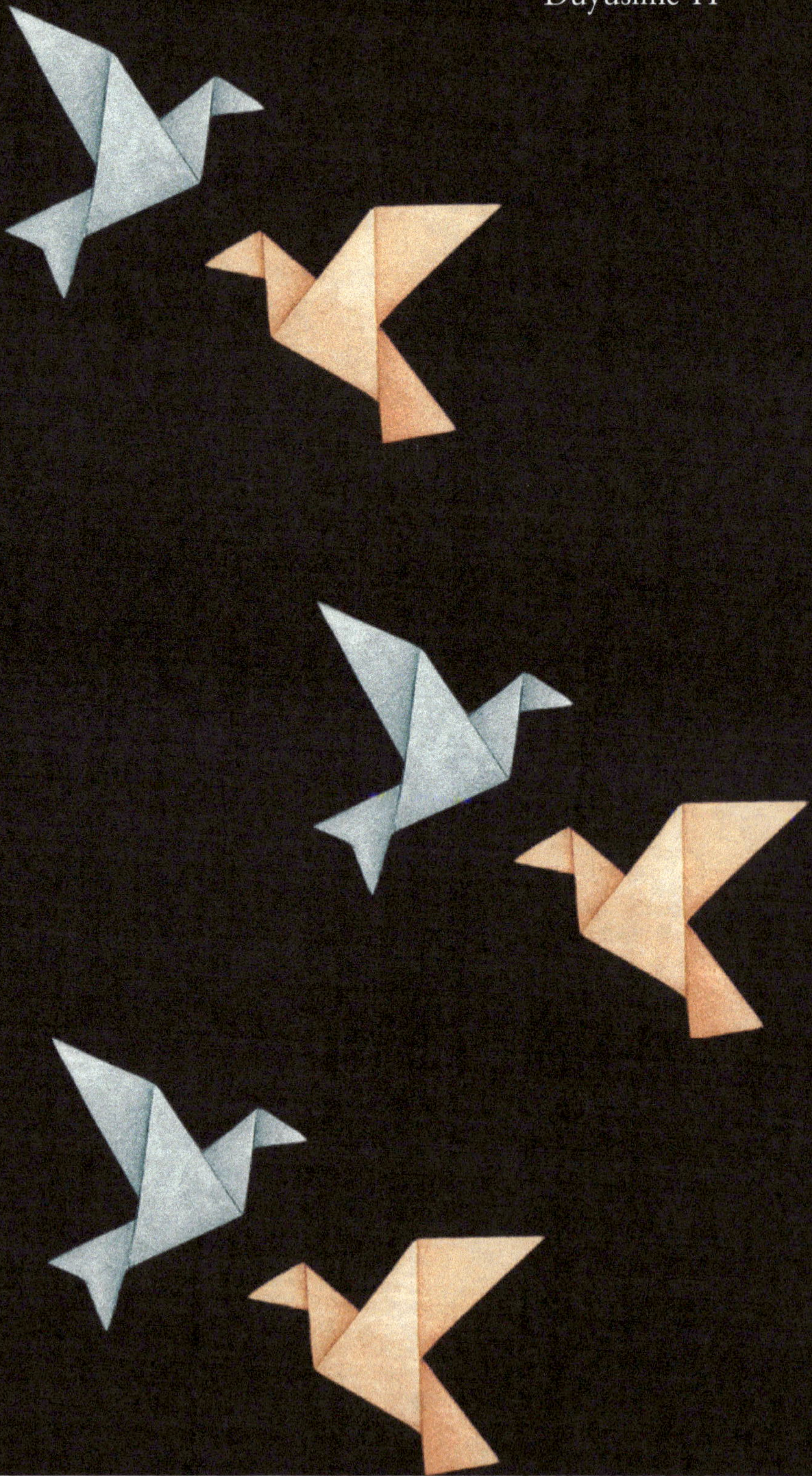

A day's work

Mentally drained like a towel wrung dry,
left hanging in the sun, stripped of every
lingering thread of thought.

Watching my shadow move through the day until
it completely disappears, Now I am alone as night
falls piecing together the day that came and left.

I should be afraid of what lingers in the dark but
I'm almost relieved The night dew will fall to add
something the day took away.

So close to giving up with nothing left then I find the strength to try again another day.

Older

Dear Mother, I am getting older. It's a scary
journey, but the scariest part is realizing how
little time I may have left with you.
My heart is heavy, refusing to move forward
until you share the pieces of your past. I see
how you love, but the distance between us
feels deeper than the ocean floor.
We speak in code, always skirting around the
words that truly need to be said. Mom, I am
getting older, and that's not an opinion, it's
the truth I dread.
I hear your voice, I see your actions, but still,
something doesn't connect. I want to ask if
you'll let me into your thoughts, even though
I already know the answer.

I fear that somewhere inside your beautiful mind,
a little girl is still screaming, trapped, unseen.
And maybe I understand that so deeply because I
am still your little girl too, trying so desperately to
rewind your tapes and make sense of the silence.
All I want is to touch the part of you that time,
pain, and silence tried to bury, before it's too late.

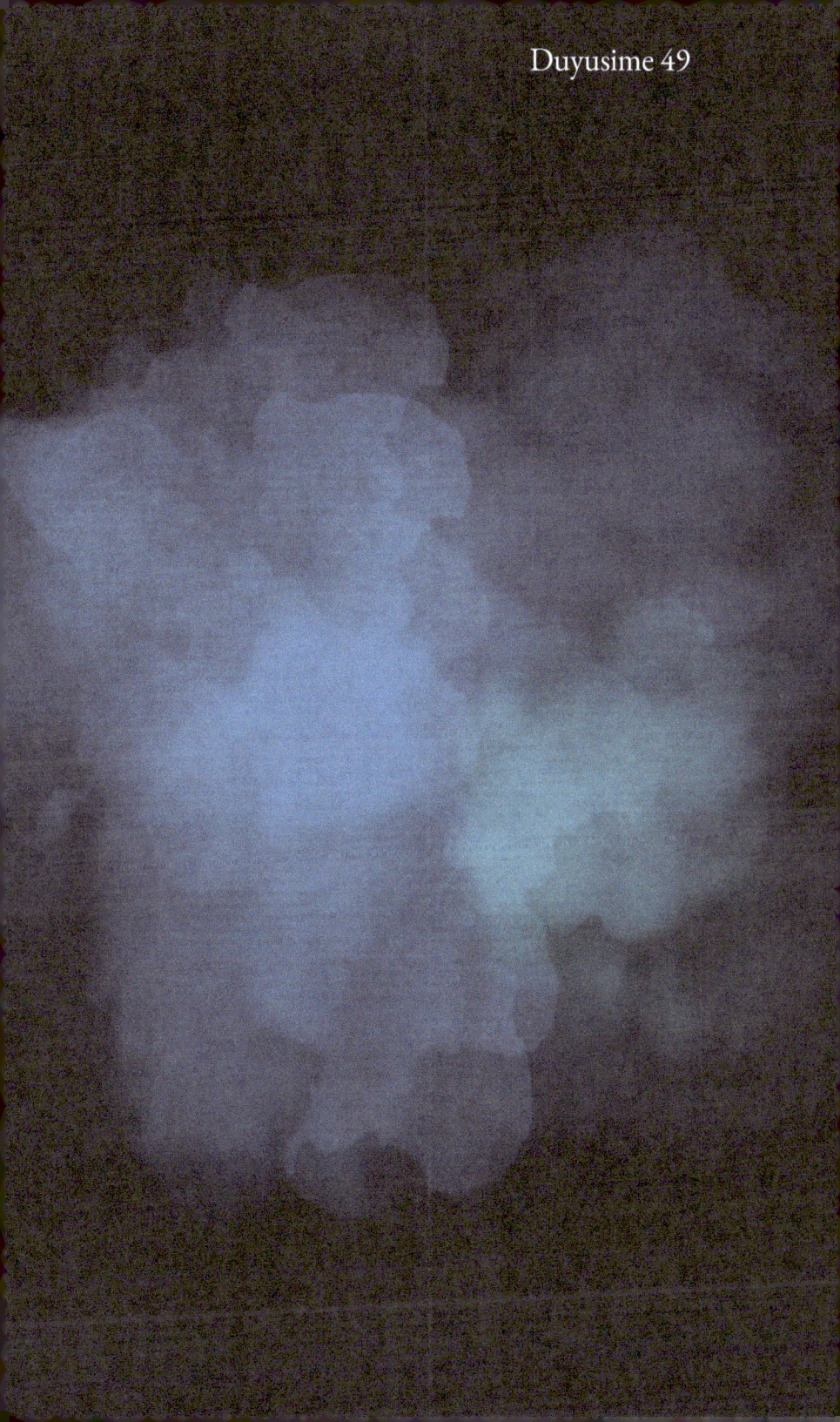

It's gets lonely

It's get lonely When the conversations start
in my head.

Background noises disappear into a pitch far
below what i can hear, The noise has sunken
but it's the silence I fear.

It gets lonely when the one I love most Cannot
understand my entirety Like who I am entirely.
Am I entitled to my feelings ?

It gets lonely when the mirror reflects your
biggest enemy.

Evenhough it is only a shell, replica of the

person still trapped inside

Cross Roads

At the end, the only thing that's left is the
journey made.

Unconscious of how I got here. The path ahead
is filled with unknown. The path behind has
only shown me pain.

So now, I sit at the crossroads. Unbound by any
tangible force, but my legs are frozen at bay.

I watch the sun rise and set in moments that feel
both rushed and still, torn inside, yet strangely at
peace

Still, I am afraid. Afraid that moving means

I've failed, but just as afraid that staying means

I've failed myself along the way

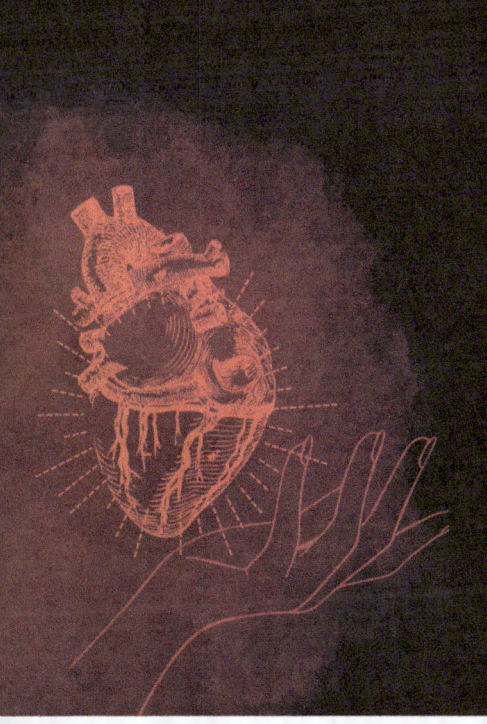

The journey

I have conquered fears that once daunted me.
I found the courage to become someone I
never imagined I could be.
Now I see that surviving in my world means
parting ways with what no longer serves me.
Who knew that facing myself would be the
most intimidating task of all?
I've taken the time to remove the layers,
peeling them back carefully, deliberately.
My existence now feels like a path, I am
meant to be on , a journey toward
understanding who I truly am.
And here I stand, metaphorically bare.

I have dug deep and uncovered a treasure long obscured by rust.

I've scratched and clawed, filing the bars down to dust. And now, looking at myself, I see two choices: remain the same or change.

Maybe this was always meant to be. My faith has led me here.

Bigger picture

Like a plane drifting through the sky,
everything below seems so small, insignificant
compared to the vastness that surrounds it.
And for a moment, I feel that same smallness,
that quiet ache of unimportance.

But somehow, it gives me peace. It gives me
courage.
Because if I am just a speck in all of this, then
maybe it's okay to live for myself. To live for
another would be madness, when I, too, am
just a fleeting part of the universe.

Broken Aesthetics

I danced externally, while internally my
wheels spun and spiraled. I forced an action
and faced an awkward emotion.

It was almost manic, this quiet scramble to
maintain control.
A performance, not for joy, but survival.
A disguise shaped to protect the aesthetic I
showed the world, carefully crafted to hide
the true conditions of my inner state.

All stars

Never let them steal your shine. The squint in your eyes when you smile is the park that will outshine all stars.

The curve in your hips is an ascension of how much your body envies your own perfection.

Don't trust yourself if you think otherwise.

The mirror will always question beauty when new standards are set. The mirrors reflect projection, enhance rejections, you are a spark. A hidden gem, mirrors know nothing of

Here's the secret: it has not mastered how to reflect your light.

Kind-hearted

Kind-hearted woman, your intention is pure. I
envy the love that lives inside you. The clock has
struck, and now it is time,
time for your scene to be seen.

Kind-hearted woman, let them watch.
They have already taken too much from you; give
no more. Stand in your light, but do not let those
snatchers tamper with your soul.

Our best

We can't heal together if we're broken in ways the other has never found guidance for. We can only rely on our best qualities, hoping we have enough remaining parts to reflect some sense of wholeness.

Just enough to teach one another how to face the problem, with patience, with presence. A bit of finesse when getting over a hurdle, and grace when we stumble along the way.

To heal together means a more profound
connection, spiritually, emotionally, but
right now, it feels severed.

I can't tell how fractured you are; I'm
blinded by my own muddle. Still, every now
and then, I get a break... and catch you
before you slip.

Fragile

When the strongest person you know breaks
it shows how fragile life is.

Fight or flight

Living in a constant state of fight or flight isn't
living at all.
Sure, I dream of flying past my limits, floating in
daydreams, untouched by the noise of the world
below.
But deep down, I still want to stay grounded.
To be present.
To see and feel the life happening around me.
Rushing into the future makes it easy to ignore
the now. It paints over the past like it never
mattered.
Everyone is fighting something.
And me? I feel like I'm at war with the world.
Fighting for something meaningful is one thing
But fighting out of fear? That's a battle I'll
never win

It's only when I let my guard down that I start
to breathe.
That I begin to accept what is.
Because I've realized, trying to control
everything is just my way of coping with what
feels unstable inside.

Figure it out

Love carried me to the finish line,
Then left me standing at the start.
What once felt strong and so divine
Unraveled slowly, fell apart.

Maybe the end was meant to show
That some beginnings help us grow.
Or maybe love, no matter how true,
Can't always be returned to you.

Gasoline

Anger feels like lighting a match in a pool of gasoline.

You are an outsider to your own wants; when it takes over, remaining is the satisfaction of watching it burn.

Anger doesn't just Destroy everything around you; it ensures you burn in the flames.

Fairytale

No one's going to rescue you; This is not a
fairytale.

This is not the tale of a girl waiting for her
knight.

The stories do not reveal the ending, only
fragments of everything before the horror.
A time prevenient to her deciding she needs
not to be saved,but to be her own knight.

Let it

Walking through lightning, telling ourselves it's just the weather. But deep down, we know we're carrying something that no longer fits in the frame.

The goal, we think, is to make sense of the mess, to tidy pain into purpose, to hang our grief like art and call it growth. But this is only the beginning.

The beginning of becoming. Of diving headfirst into an ocean of experience that doesn't wait for you to breathe.

Some waves feel like entire worlds collapsing. Let them. Drown the remains in your tears if you must.

Because no matter how steady your hands are, you can't force a cracked frame to hold something it was never made for.

So let it rip. Let it tear through the canvas you painted with borrowed colors. Let it shred the storyline you outgrew in silence. Let it rip until what's left is real. Until what's left is finally, you.

So let it rip. Let it tear through the canvas you painted with borrowed colors. Let it shred the storyline you outgrew in silence. Let it rip until what's left is real. Until what's left is finally, you.

Not personal

I can no longer tolerate mediocrity in my life.
It would be a setback to welcome into my peace all
the things I've finally found the courage to let go.

I cannot ration what little I have left.
My personal choice is not a personal diss to your
struggle.
The truth is, I know nothing about your story.
So when I say I refuse to let you into my gates,
into my sacred space,
just listen.

Your energy exists in a time and space
that no longer aligns with mine.
I will not carve myself into smaller pieces
just to make you fit.

I will not feed your ego
just to justify why I choose to keep you out.
You've shown that your spirit has not healed.
And as a token to the girl
who has given all she could give
I love you dearly,
but I choose my peace.

Past is Present

The past is the present, the fiction lies here. We tell ourselves it's gone, that time moves on in one direction, but memory has no resect for the clock. Take a look.

Not a glance, but a real look. Through a magnifying glass. Zoom in on the fragments, the minuscule particles that lie dormant, invisible to the naked eye but never truly gone.

The deeper you go, the more undeniable it becomes.

The past doesn't vanish. It embeds itself in the fibers of who we are. It whispers in decisions, echoes in pauses, repeats itself in the patterns we swore we'd break.

The past is not behind us. It is a conjunction of light and lens, a fusion of what was and what is seen. Light, when it hits just right, divulges the details we tried to bury. It paints the unseen. It reveals the residue. The fingerprints. The traces.

The past is now. In darkness, lenses have no purpose. You can't focus on what you refuse to shine a light on. But now, now is the present. Now is the gift. Eyes open. Wounds uncovered. Truth rising.

The present belongs to those brave enough to search. To ask the questions. To hold the mirror. To dissect the narrative and rewrite the meaning.

So don't be fooled, the past never left. It lives in tone, in hesitation, in dreams we didn't pursue because something way back told us we weren't enough.

But here's the shift: when you bring the light, the lens regains its purpose. When you stop fearing the fragments, they show you the full picture.

You're not trapped by what was. You're illuminated by what is, if you dare to look.

Because the past is present. And the present is yours to define.

www.ingramcontent.com/pod-product-compliance
Lightning Source LLC
Chambersburg PA
CBHW070444130626
46553CB00006B/2286

* 9 7 9 8 2 1 8 1 9 9 1 3 5 *